write away

primary

Senior Editor: Heather Neill
Project Editor: Jenny Siklós

Managing Editor: Patricia Grogan

Art Editor: Nicola Liddiard
Teachers' Notes: Angel Scott
Discussion notes: Lorraine Dawes and Angel Scott

First published in Great Britain in 2000 by TSL Education Limited
Admiral House, 66-68 East Smithfield, London E1W 1BX

A CIP catalogue record for this book is available from the British Library

ISBN 1-84122-018-3

Colour reproduction by Prima Creative Services, UK
Printed and bound in Belgium by Proost

Foreword

When people contact The TES about Write Away, they still sometimes refer to it as the Children's Literacy Project. This was never its title; the intention among TES staff, and our partners in the National Association for the Teaching of English and McDonald's Restaurants Ltd., was always to celebrate young people's creativity and the inspiration provided by their teachers. We are, however, as aware as anyone how much time and energy schools spend on raising standards of literacy and we could not be more delighted if Write Away is serving this purpose as well.

Write Away: the Children's Literary Project seems to have struck a chord with teachers all over the country and some as far away as Portugal, Switzerland and even Japan. The first booklet was given away in The *TES* in the summer of 1997. As a result 10,000 children entered the associated competition and many schools reported that they were happy to keep it in their repertoire of resources. The following two booklets, in 1998 and 1999, proved equally popular. Each time we received 10,000 entries and celebrated with the 20 winners at Shakespeare's Globe in London.

The popularity of Write Away is not surprising: many of the liveliest children's authors have contributed specially commissioned autobiographical pieces to the three booklets and, in 1998 and 1999, to the *TES* Primary magazine. Jan Mark, Michael Morpurgo, Michael Rosen, Janni Howker, Kit Wright, Grace Nichols, Raymond Briggs, Helen Cresswell, Farrukh Dhondy, Beverley Naidoo and Philip Pullman are just a few of the favourite writers represented. As the work by young people flooded in we were delighted to publish some outstanding examples of that as well.

Now the pieces most suitable for Primary readers are gathered together for the first time, along with a new contribution from Jacqueline Wilson, one of this age group's most popular authors. Angel Scott, lecturer in English education at the University of Durham and experienced teacher, has provided a brand new introduction, full of ideas for teaching autobiography, to expand on the more specific notes which accompany each piece. With the exception of the notes for Jacqueline Wilson's story, which are provided by Angel Scott, these are written by Lorraine Dawes, English and Literacy Co-ordinator for the London Borough of Redbridge. At the back of the book you will find details of other work by the professional authors featured in these pages.

A companion volume is available for older readers.

Write Away!

Heather Neill,
Arts Editor,
The Times Educational Supplement

Teachers' notes

This anthology of autobiographical writing with teaching ideas arose out of the TES/NATE/McDonald's very successful Write Away competitions. Included here are five of the prize-winning pieces by primary school pupils, the six specially-commissioned pieces written by well-known children's authors and one piece newly commissioned for this book. With the accompanying posters, this book is a valuable resource for teaching autobiographical writing. It provides:

- models of good writing which form the basis for genre study during shared and guided reading
- resources and teaching ideas for developing first person writing and particularly autobiography for shared, guided and independent writing
- practical suggestions to help children become more effective writers of extended writing
- information about relevant, suitable books written by the authors to encourage wider reading for pleasure

The National Literacy Strategy is based on the principle that reading and writing develop together and that children need to be taught to read as writers and write as readers. In order to be fluent and efficient readers, children need to understand about different text types and their different features. The teaching emphasis is on structure and language features and is best done during shared reading when children can be introduced to the text type and become familiarised to its key features by the teacher demonstrating and using texts to model and explain. Children can investigate the text type through reading at shared, guided and independent time. Once children are familiar with a specific text type they can then move on to using it in their own writing. This process can begin in shared writing with the teacher demonstrating and defining the conventions at word, sentence and text level. Through shared writing, children can then begin to imitate and experiment with the text type drawing on their reading experience. Finally, through guided and independent writing, children can begin to apply and develop the writing skills needed for that text type. Opportunities will need to be provided for extended independent writing outside the Literacy Hour.

By reading and analysing the examples of writing in this anthology, pupils will learn the language characteristics of autobiographical writing. Autobiography is one of the most accessible forms of writing because although it is non-fiction, it is still narrative in form.

Autobiography is writing a story about yourself. It is based on fact and real experience. The main character is the writer so it is written in the first person. The story is about key incidents in the writer's life. It describes the main influences – people, places, events – on the writer. It describes interactions between the writer and important people in his or her life. It shows the writer's feelings, thoughts, reactions and beliefs. By reading the writing of others and understanding the genre, pupils will be able to use these features in their own writing.
The posters are designed to help pupils understand the general characteristics of autobiographical writing and examples are given drawn from the pieces of writing in the anthology. Pupils can look at the pieces in the light of these characteristics and see how the writer has used them to create an interesting account. The posters and the pieces of writing can be used for shared reading.

Getting started on writing

Once they have understood the characteristics of autobiographical writing from shared, guided and independent reading of the examples in the anthology, pupils then need to be supported in producing their own writing.

Finding something to write about is the first hurdle for many children. Focusing on events that the writers have experienced, rather than drawing exclusively on their imagination, allows them to concentrate on the writing skills. Having first-hand experience of the event helps them to recreate it and bring it alive for the reader through using language vividly. Reading the autobiographical accounts of other people triggers memories and provides interesting discussions which can lead into writing.

The writing process

If children are to write well they need to be taught about the writing process as well as the range of purposes, audiences and forms of writing. They need support, time and encouragement to get it right. Good writing does not just come from thinking and working on paper or screen; pupils need to read good writing and to talk about what makes it good. Writers need sympathetic and supportive listeners while they are planning and composing. They need to test out ideas. While they are revising, they need to hear what their writing sounds like and to see how it affects others.

Children need to understand the importance of writing developing through stages from planning to presentation, where appropriate. Writing autobiography, like all forms of extended writing, needs time and effort. Children should be encouraged to ask questions like: how am I going to write about it? What kind of writing is it going to be? What kind of language will I use? How will I bring the incident alive for my readers? This will involve them in thinking at word, sentence and text level about style and sentence structure, vocabulary, dialogue, description, imagery; writing in the first person; whether to write in the past tense or the present.

Working with children on the writing process

In the early stages of planning and drafting, children need support. Feedback from the teacher in these initial stages can significantly improve pupils' work. Discussing children's writing with them is often more helpful than taking it away to mark. Allowing the children to read their writing out loud, and discussing the content first, encourages them to think about what they are saying as well as how they say it.

Correcting the writing can form part of the discussion about the importance of tackling writing in stages so that they can concentrate on composing at the planning and drafting stage, and accuracy and appropriateness at revising and proofreading stages. If they are encouraged to think that all aspects of the writing process are important, this may help them to see the point of working in stages.

Ways of working in the classroom

Supporting the children as they write can only be accomplished in group time in guided writing where there are opportunities for continuing dialogue about structure, style, purpose and so on. Guided writing sessions can provide support for children preparing to write, while they are drafting and afterwards when responding to written work. This is more specifically outlined in the teaching sequences from the National Literacy Strategy Training module on Writing (DfEE, 1999 – available from The National Centre for Literacy and Numeracy on 0118 952 7531/2).

Writing frames can help children with structuring what they want to say and using the language features of this text type in their own writing. A carefully-selected series of starter sentences can provide a framework for the pupil. The framework should help the pupil work with the language features of autobiographical writing.

All the pieces will benefit from being read aloud and discussed as models of good autobiographical writing. Children could also read and discuss them in group time with and without teacher support. Discussion can take place in pairs or groups as well as a whole class. The activities for each piece have two aims: to focus on the writing and techniques that the writer has used and to provide support for the pupils' own writing.

The final product

Presenting their work is an important aspect of writing. Using a word processor makes the writing look more professional than handwriting. Working on screen makes it easier to redraft and proof-read. Providing an audience for the children's writing is also important and there are many opportunities: a school magazine, a class book, a school book, a school/class display, a presentation for assembly or parents, or a display for open day.

My Mum's Ring

I didn't know anything about this ring. I only knew I threw it out the window because he told me. I was only three when I did it!

Michael Rosen

Have you noticed that some parents forget the naughty things you do, and others remember *everything*?

My mum used to forget, but my dad was the one who remembered things.

If I did something bad he'd say, 'Oh yes, like the time you threw your mother's ring out of the window – it was her grandmother's.'

I didn't know anything about this ring. I only knew I threw it out the window because he told me. I was only three when I did it!

So I'd do something wrong. Like sticking the top off the toothpaste in his shaving soap.

I was day-dreaming that the toothpaste was treasure. Buried treasure...and one day pirates would come and find it...and dig it up...

And so I left the top off the toothpaste buried in my dad's shaving soap.

Next day, mum says, 'Anyone seen the top off the toothpaste?'

My brother says, 'Nope!'

'Michael?'

'Nope.'

My dad says, 'Typical! No one knows!'

Meanwhile, every day he uses the shaving soap, until one day he suddenly finds, poking out of the soap – the top off the toothpaste.

He walks into the kitchen. He comes over to my brother. 'Why is the top off the toothpaste in my shaving soap?'

And my brother says, 'I don't know.'

And he comes over to me, holding out the jar – 'Why is the top off the toothpaste in the shaving soap?'

And I said, 'I don't know.'

But when I said it my eyebrows went up in the air.

'The eyebrows. I can see you're lying. What did you think you were doing sticking the top off the toothpaste in my shaving soap?'

And I said, 'Er - buried treasure. Er - I thought pirates would come and find it.'

And he looked at me and said, 'Oh yes, like the time you threw your mother's ring out of the window – it was her grandmother's.'

My dad remembered *everything*.

write away

Ted Dewan

Discussion points

After hearing the story read aloud, read it to yourself a few times and discuss it with others.

Sense of immediacy: This story sounds as though the author is speaking to you directly. How does he achieve this?
Tenses: Some of this story is written in the past tense and some in the present. What effect does this have on the reader?
Emotion and humour: Act out the story in pairs. Try saying the lines of dialogue in an exaggerated way, like people having a family argument. How do we know how the author and his dad feel?
Structure: Notice how the author begins and ends the story and how he sets out the dialogue, with a new line for each new speaker.

Writing suggestions:
Michael Rosen's stories and poems usually remind us of our own family anecdotes. Think about similar situations that have happened in your life. Is there something you once did that you are reminded of every time you do something wrong? Try to recall the exact words said to you.

In pairs, tell each other your stories. You might like to try acting them out.

Think about the opening line of your story. You may want to link it with the ending, as Michael Rosen did. Then draft the dialogue, as though you were telling someone else.

If you need to, refer back to the story to see how to set out the dialogue with new lines and punctuation marks.

About the author...

When asked how the writing process works for him, Michael Rosen said: 'Writing involves a special kind of concentration. In a funny sort of way, you have to turn your eyes round and look into yourself. This isn't only because you might be writing about yourself; it's a way of conjuring up pictures, phrases, words, stories, scenes, characters, rhymes, rhythms and all that.'

Pipe Dreams

Kit Wright

Not many people nowadays smoke a pipe.

My father did.

And he wasn't the only one. Many people smoked pipes of different shapes and sizes, from the ones that stuck out straight from the mouth, to the ones that bent like a slow snake. Well, they all seemed to like it, somehow, smoking a pipe.

For instance, I can remember a barge full of coal come chuntering down the Grand Union. That was the old canal beside whose banks we went to school. And steering this barge from the back was an old lady... her teeth clamped hard around a pipe! But nobody seemed to like it as much as my father. He puffed on it in the morning and he puffed on it in the evening. And if his pipe was already lit, he puffed on it in the lavatory. And this is my story.

One day he dropped his pipe down the lavatory bowl. Well! You'd think he might have thrown it away. Yuck! But no... this was a favourite pipe. So he picked it up, and he washed it out, and he soaked it for seven days in disinfectant. He soaked it so long the bowl of his pipe turned a kind of rusty green. But it was clean! So he took it out and he filled it. And he lit it. Well, I wasn't there, but my brother was. He told me what happened next.

A giant green flame came leaping out of my father's pipe. It burnt the ceiling and scorched his eyebrows. And apparently it didn't taste too good. 'Good God!' he cried, as he sprang up from his chair. 'Good God in Heaven!', and he danced round the room before throwing his pipe in the fire. Which just goes to show that a week's disinfectant is not the best thing to put in your pipe. Even if it's a favourite one.

One of my father's friends was called Clarence. Now Clarence didn't smoke a pipe: what he did was take snuff. Little pinches of it from a tin that was always in his pocket.

Clarence took a good deal of snuff. And on the way from the tin to his nostrils a lot of it spilled on his clothes. In fact Clarence's clothes usually looked as though he'd been rolling on the ground in them. And once I did actually see him on the floor.

Poor Clarence suffered from very bad rheumatism, something he never complained about. He walked on two sticks and one day lost his footing and went crashing down. Everyone was appalled and rushed to his aid.

'Clarrie, are you hurt?' cried my father.

But Clarence lay on the floor, smiling.

'I'm fine,' he said. 'Sorry about the disturbance.'

And he got his tin out and took a pinch of snuff!

One day he dropped his pipe down the lavatory bowl. Well! You'd think he might have thrown it away. Yuck! But no... this was a favourite pipe.

write away

Discussion points

After hearing the piece read aloud, read it to yourself a few times and discuss it with others.

Comment and observation: This piece of writing is about people other than the author, but is full of personal observation. Look through the story and pick out the phrases and sentences that tell us what the author thinks about the people and events he is describing. Notice the way these are written.

Style: Look at the opening, and consider how effective it is. Observational pieces like this need to leap straight in, and the layout of these opening statements draws the reader in.

Content: It is interesting how objects can prompt recollections about people and events. Conversations are often full of anecdotes. With others, think of things that might prompt stories, like bicycles, dogs, mealtimes, and so on, and see what anecdotes come up.

Writing Suggestions:
You may want to write up anecdotes related to a single subject, as the writer has done in this piece. Remember to include your observations as well as the events themselves. Use a response partner to gain feedback on your first draft – is there anything that is unclear? Questions asked by your partner can prompt you to reply with words and phrases that will enhance your writing further.

About the author...

Kit Wright says of the writing process: 'I mainly write poetry, an art that may be practised in many other places than behind a desk. I always carry a notebook with me and often scribble down ideas, overheard dialogue, rhymes and phrases while sitting on the top of a bus. On train journeys, or sitting in the pub, I've been known to compose whole poems. This is just as well as my desk is usually so cluttered it's hard to find a space for writing!

Shane McGowan

Secrets

Helen Cresswell

The first secret of my childhood was what I called my 'pretty things'. It was a secret hoard of treasure. In my room was a doll's bed, wooden and painted blue and with its own little mattress. Under that mattress was a perfect hiding place for all the small objects I would collect. My mother must have thought we had Borrowers in the house when things began to go missing – a little silver dish, a string of coloured beads, a tiny purse of soft blue leather. One day, at a friend's house, we went through her mother's dressing table and found the most beautiful thing ever – a slim, round box of mother-of-pearl, deliciously scented by the face powder it held.

I took it home and hid it under the mattress with the rest of my hoard. From time to time I would go to my room, shut the door and take out my treasures one by one to gaze at and enjoy.

But the mother-of-pearl powder compact was a treasure too far. It was missed, and I was soon found out as the culprit. In tears I led the way to my room, the mattress was lifted and my secret hoard was laid bare. The grown ups used the word 'stealing'. What I had been doing, I was told, was wicked. And I had thought I was simply collecting pretty things.

After that, I found a hollow in the stone wall of our front garden, half hidden by the privet hedge, a miniature Aladdin's cave. In it I hid only the tiniest things – sea shells and tiny fragments of coloured glass, red, green, amber, blue. These I found lying in the roughly made roads around our house – all through my childhood the town was spreading, eating up the countryside. I still wonder about those glass jewels, how they came to be there. Sometimes I am tempted to go back and search for the hollow stone in the wall and see if my secret treasure is still there.

I had other secrets, too. The recurring nightmare of a vast underground cavern, where in the darkness a pair of green eyes glowed, the discovery that words were like music, and could sing and fall into patterns called poetry. But the greatest secret of all happened out of the blue one day in summer, when I think I was nine or ten years old.

I was walking alone (children could, in those days) down a very long, straight suburban road. Either side were the stiff and starchy houses with their neat gardens and clipped hedges. Then it happened.

I stop, and I stand stockstill. The tar on the road is melting, I can smell it. The world about me is suddenly foreign. I think: 'This is not real'. I think it and I know it. Then: 'I don't belong here. What am I doing here?' I think it and I know it. It is at once terrifying and comforting. At that moment the boundaries of reality are shifted, once and forever. I have a new secret treasure and it is hidden not under a mattress, or in a hole in the wall, but within my own self.

And I spend the rest of my life writing, writing to find out the mystery that lies behind what most people call 'reality', and what I am doing here. I explore the other world I glimpsed in books like The Night-watchmen and The Bongleweed. It was the secret I discovered that hot day long ago that made me the kind of writer I am.

I stop, and I stand stockstill. The tar on the road is melting, I can smell it. The world about me is suddenly foreign. I think: 'This is not real'.

write away

About the author...

When asked how the writing process works for her, Helen Cresswell says: 'I have to write facing into the light. I write everything by hand using a real fountain pen with ink in it. For timeless or historical passages, I use sepia ink in an ivory pen; for modern or funny passages I have a scarlet pen with black ink.

Sarah Symonds

Discussion points

After hearing the piece read aloud, read it to yourself a few times and discuss it with others.

The 'voice': The author confides her secrets to us, conveying the emotions that she felt as well as the events, capturing our interest and making us want to understand the 'greatest secret' revealed at the end. What do you make of her greatest secret? Talk about what 'the boundaries of reality are shifted' means to you. How does this relate to other Helen Cresswell stories that you know?

Description and detail: Throughout the story, description is grounded in the senses: how things looked, smelt, felt. Find examples and talk about them.

Being a writer: This is one of those rare stories that give us insight into the mind of a writer. Do you think similar experiences of 'glimpsing other worlds' happen to other writers?

I stayed silent about Garry at first, but I told one of the nice ladies at playgroup. I was surprised at her reaction. I expected her to laugh or tell me not to be silly.

Friends

Rosie Seager

I was never really a lonely child. In fact, I had a lot of close friends. There were Kate, John, Peter, Jone, Lauren and Sarah. It doesn't sound many, but I was only little. So I don't know why I needed an imaginary friend.

I was about three when it started. I began to imagine that I had another friend called Garry. I kept it to myself at first, only telling my sister and my mother, who told my father.

It all started when I had a dream. I dreamt that I had a new friend called Garry, and when I woke up he was sitting right beside me. He followed me everywhere. I burst into my sister's bedroom. 'Holly, look, this is Garry, my new best friend.'

Holly was getting changed for school and shooed me out, telling me not to be silly. After that I kept it to myself, only playing with Garry when I was alone. Only I could see him. I couldn't understand why no one else could. We did everything together: ate our breakfast, played around the farm and had our naps together.

I then started playgroup. I stayed silent about Garry at first, but I told one of the nice ladies at playgroup. I was surprised at her reaction. I expected her to laugh or tell me not to be silly. So you can imagine my surprise when she said, 'Oh really, dear, what's his name?'

I told her and she replied, 'Well you and Garry can go and sit on the carpet with a book, and I'll get some drinks.' She then brought in a huge tray piled with chocolate digestives and cups of milk. There was an extra drink and biscuit for Garry. So my imaginary friend was included in everything.

One day my mother went away and stayed a few days. When she finally returned home she had a special surprise. It was a baby boy! He was called Harry. I was really excited at first, but then I no longer had any attention. When people came round they came to see Harry, not me. I became number 2 instead of number 1. Harry was taking over. I was feeling more and more left out. I started using this as an excuse to play with Garry.

I left playgroup and the nice ladies who understood me, and started school – a brand new world, new smells, new sounds. I was lost. I couldn't play with Garry. I had to sit next to a boy who smelled funny and always had a runny nose. It was awful. I started to play on my own with Garry, leaving my other friends behind.

Harry moved into my room, and I had to share with my sister. We had bunk beds. I couldn't play with Garry any more. Nothing was private. I became naughty and blamed everything on Garry. My mother got angry and told me to stop being stupid. I was angry because no one would listen to me.

One day I woke up with an empty space beside me. I looked around calling Garry's name. I was frantically searching my room when my mother walked in. 'I can't find Garry, mum – he's gone.' I said desperately, with tears in my eyes. She sat down and said soothingly, 'Look Rosie, he was just a made-up friend. You're growing up. I'm so sorry, love.'

Garry came back in a dream that night. But only to say goodbye. Just as quickly as he had appeared, he disappeared. Just like that.

write away

Discussion points

After hearing the piece read aloud, read it to yourself a few times and discuss it with others.

This story gives us insight into how real an imaginary friend can seem: the way he was 'sitting right beside me' and the loss felt at the 'empty space' when he had gone. The author takes us right back to a young child's mind, with the tension between having an imaginary friend and being aware of others' dismissal of him summed up in the repeated sentence 'I couldn't play with Garry'.

The author speaks directly to the reader. Notice the opening sentences and, later, 'So you can imagine my surprise...'.

Many stories are based on a character that not everyone can see. You could take these characters and develop a story about them; or maybe you can recall a similar friend in your own childhood.

About the author...

Rosie says she only thought of Garry again 'when I was asked to write about something I remembered'. English is certainly one of her favourite subjects: 'I'm better at indoor things like writing than outdoor things like sports,' she says. 'Writing,' she says, 'is a career I'd like to pursue, especially stories for children.' She is a student at Whitchurch Community College, Whitchurch, Buckinghamshire.

David Hitch

A Bunch of Flowers

Eimear O'Brien

My Daddy is not what you would call 'the romantic type'. He's more the solid 'down-to-earth' type. My Mammy says, 'Your Daddy has his feet so firmly on the ground, they're actually a little bit below the ground.'

I don't know what she means by that, but I do know he's no Tom Cruise. When I tell him he should buy Mammy a big bunch of red roses for Valentine's Day, he just laughs and says, 'Sure, your mother knew what she was getting before she married me. Wouldn't I look a real sissy buying a bunch of flowers and everybody in Magherafelt laughing at me!'

Well, I remember a time when Daddy bought Mammy a big bunch of flowers. About six years ago, Mammy got very sick and she stayed in bed and she did not go to work. Sometimes she cried. One day I came home from school with my brother and sister and Mammy was in hospital.

When we went into the hospital to see her, she was lying in bed with a drip on her arm. She called the drip Fred, and she told me not to worry. I started to cry and asked her if she was going to die. She said she was not. She was going to have a baby.

At 4 o'clock, in Granny's house, the phone rang and Daddy told us that we had a new baby sister called Aisling.

Mammy was only allowed to come home from the hospital if she promised to stay in bed. So she came home and stayed in bed for months and months and months. Every week the doctor came to see her and he gave her injections which made her even sicker.

Sometimes I heard her whispering to Daddy, 'Do you think it will be all right, Seamus?' And Daddy would say, 'Certainly it will, with the help of God.'

On the 10th September 1992, Daddy told us that when we came home from school, Granny would give us our dinner and mind us until he came home from the hospital. At 4 o'clock, in Granny's house, the phone rang and Daddy told us that we had a new baby sister called Aisling.

Two days later, Ciaran, Claire and I were all going to the hospital to visit Mammy and Aisling. On the way, Daddy stopped at a florist's shop and he bought the biggest, pinkest bunch of flowers I have ever seen. They were all tied up with an enormous pink bow. When we went into the hospital, Daddy carried this great bunch of flowers and he did not seem to care who saw him. He was not even a wee bit embarrassed. I don't understand adults, do you?

Sarah Symonds

write away

About the author...

Eimear's story is about a family incident which also involves her teacher. At the time she wrote this, Eimear's English teacher at St Mary's Grammar School, Magherafelt, Co. Derry, Northern Ireland, was her mother, Shelagh. She says Eimear has a 'piercing memory' of the moment in 1992 described in the story when the five-year-old asked her: 'Are you going to die?' and she replied: 'No, I'm going to have a baby.' Shelagh remarks: 'She was always a very direct child.'

Discussion points

After hearing the piece read aloud, read it to yourself a few times and discuss it with others.

It is interesting to explore why Daddy wasn't embarrassed about flowers on that occasion. Has the idea of what others think ever stopped you doing something? Or has there been an occasion when you've gone ahead and done what you wanted to anyway?

It is also interesting to see how the author introduces her father in the opening of the story, and how she includes what her mother says about him. It is a very effective opening which helps us get to know both characters.

Notice how the issue of the flowers frames this story of a sister's birth. Maybe an event in your life was made more memorable by something that was done or said unexpectedly.

Here be Dragons

That thrill is there still, whenever I open a new notebook, and look at the glorious blank pages. Anything is possible.

Adèle Geras

When I was nine, I lived with my parents in what is now called Sabah, but which we knew as North Borneo.

At the bottom of our garden there was a beach that looked like a Bounty advertisement. The only school was a hut made of bamboo and palm leaves, and it was up on stilts, because during the rainy season, water fell from the sky in torrents. From my bedroom window I could see: the road, my friend Toni's house, a field, and then the huge, purple bulk of Mount Kinabalu.

One day, the newspaper, The Sabah Times, announced a competition for children. They would give a Parker '51 pen-and-pencil set to the person who wrote the best story called: 'The Legend of Kinabalu'. Also, they would publish it in the paper, and in 1953, a Parker '51 was the most luxurious pen in the world.

My Dad was very encouraging. He brought me special paper from his office. It was beautiful. Each sheet had blue lines to write on, a pink margin and a neat little hole in the top left-hand corner.

Perhaps it was too beautiful because at first I couldn't think what to write. I discussed the mountain with everyone I knew and they told me this: there was a dragon living at the top. That was all I needed. I thought of a tale full of adventures and excitement. It had princes and princesses in it, and the dragon was guarding the treasure. The story ended with my scaly creature chasing the baddies from the mountain, toasting and roasting them with his fiery breath.

After I'd sent it in, I spent my days hoping and worrying. Most of the time I could close my eyes and imagine my words all laid out in the paper, but sometimes I saw my pages being scrunched up and the editor throwing them into the waste-paper basket.

I won't keep you in suspense, dear readers. I won the competition and my story appeared on the front page of the newspaper. I treasured my Parker set for years and years, but lost it at boarding-school. I can remember exactly what it looked like.

After my Dad died, I found my story among his papers. The yellow cutting from *The Sabah Times* nearly fell apart as I unfolded it. I was reminded of how happy I'd been to win, but even better, how much I'd loved conjuring up dragons, princesses, stolen treasure and an enormous purple mountain. That thrill is there still, whenever I open a new notebook, and look at the glorious blank pages. Anything is possible.

write away

Ted Dewan

Discussion points

After hearing the story read aloud, read it to yourself a few times and discuss it with others.

The 'voice': The author could be talking to the readers. What sentences and phrases give the impression she is speaking?

Description/detail: Writers of autobiography often describe things in a personal way. Look at the second and fourth paragraphs and discuss the ways in which the author describes her home and the writing paper.

Emotions: List the writer's emotions and the phrases that describe them.

Writing suggestions:

The story might remind you of a competition you entered and won or lost, or it may remind you of something you did, wrote, drew or made that your parents treasured, or about which you feel proud.

Try to remember that time and feel the emotions you felt then. Picture the scene as you saw it. Think of things you said and thought. Drawing or doodling words may help.

You may want to tell someone your story before you start drafting it, or you may want to build it in your mind silently. It may be helpful to imagine a listener or reader as you write. People are always interested to hear personal stories.

Try drafting on a computer. Then you can add in thoughts and move the text as you wish. If drafting on paper, write on every other line, so you can add things.

When redrafting, think about how well your own voice is creating pictures in the readers' minds, and letting them know how you felt.

About the author...

Adèle Geras says of the writing process and why she likes writing: 'I write my books straight on to the computer. I write very quickly once I get going, though I think of all sorts of excuses to delay the moment when I have to start working. I like writing because:

1) I can pretend to be anyone I like, and take part in all kinds of lives as well as my real one.

2) I can travel anywhere I want without moving out of my seat.

3) I can use language to paint pictures.'

My Two Aunties

Raymond Briggs

When the war began I was five years old and had been evacuated to Dorset. Here I lived with two elderly aunties in a small stone cottage in the country. The walls were over two feet thick and the stone stairs curved steeply up beside the fireplace. The ceilings were so low that you could stand on the bottom stair and put something on the bedroom floor. The tiny bedroom windows were at knee level.

There was no telephone, no television, no tapes or CDs, no computer, no car, no shower, no bathroom, no central heating, no running hot water. Baths were taken in a tin tub in the kitchen. Except for the one coal fire in the living room there was no heating at all.

The lavatory was a corrugated iron shed under the apple tree. It did not flush. Inside it was a metal bucket containing disinfectant. It was called an Elsan. Mr Blake, a very poor farmer, used to be paid to come in and empty it once a month. He dug a hole and buried the contents under the apple tree. You were not allowed to pee in the Elsan as it would have filled up too quickly. I had to pee in the hedge.

The aunties always kept three suitcases ready-packed in case of invasion. If the Germans invaded we would have to flee westwards as refugees. One night, amid the drone of bombers overhead, there came a sudden roar of engines and a deafening burst of machine gun fire. It sounded very close.

Aunt Betty shrieked, 'Get the cases, Flo!' We hurried downstairs, pulled on coats over our pyjamas and nightdresses, seized the suitcases and stood there trembling. Quite where we were going, on foot, in the middle of the winter night, was not clear.

In the end, we went nowhere and returned to bed, unharmed but very frightened.

Once a week, a bus came through the village about a mile away. We used to walk down to catch this bus and go into Shaftesbury to the shops. A big treat was to go to the pictures afterwards, but we always had to leave before the film ended, in order to catch the one and only bus home.

It was on one of these shopping trips that I committed a dreadful offence which still embarrasses me today. I had lost a little toy in the garden and was very upset, as I'd paid sixpence for it. I even cried. Kind Auntie Flo said, 'Never mind, dear. I'll get you something next week.' So next Saturday she bought me a little toy costing fourpence. I can still remember walking along the pavement beside her and wrestling with my conscience as I looked down at the pavement going past under my feet. I knew it was wrong, but I had to say it. 'You owe me tuppence!' I blurted out, and blushed with shame even as I said it. What a vile, ungrateful little beast I must have been!

Of course, I am much nicer today.

I knew it was wrong, but I had to say it. 'You owe me tuppence!' I blurted out, and blushed with shame even as I said it.

Discussion points

After hearing the piece read aloud, read it to yourself a few times and discuss it with others.

The 'voice': Events that are remembered from early childhood are the events that had the greatest impact on us at the time. Talk about the aspects of life with his aunts that are remembered in this piece of writing – why do you think they have stuck in the author's mind?

Description and detail: In first-person writing, effective description is often written through the author's first-hand experience: we can really picture the low ceilings and the bedroom windows of the cottage. Find other examples of vivid description.

Comments and judgments: In the last paragraph, the author reflects on an incident that still embarrasses him today. 'I knew it was wrong, but I had to say it.' Can you bring to mind any similar incidents in your life where you were ashamed or embarrassed about something you had said?

Conveying feelings: When the author describes his feelings at the time, he uses 'blurted' and 'blushed' and describes how he 'looked down at the pavement going past'. Do you agree that including how he spoke and moved adds to the description of how he felt? Brainstorm some feelings, and for each one think of verbs that could describe how a person would speak and move if they were feeling that way – acting it out may help.

Writing suggestions:
This story may remind you of a time when you lived far away from home, or make you recall a time when you had mixed feelings. You may want to tell someone else your story before you write it, or build it silently in your mind. Try drafting on a computer. Then you can add in thoughts and move text as you wish. If drafting on paper, try writing on every other line, so you can add things. When redrafting, think about how well you have used your first-hand experience in describing the setting.

write away

About the author...

When asked how the writing process works for him, Raymond Briggs said: 'I write with an italic fountain pen. I don't use a computer – I don't even type. I like writing on trains: there is just enough discraction to concentrate the mind. The writing always comes first; the pictures go on in my head. It's rather like film writing. When the script is in some sort of form, I become a director, then a costume and scene designer. Then I cram it into a book and become a book designer.'

David Bromley

At home that evening I remembered the graffiti and asked my parents about them. They said those were very rude words for black people. That's when I discovered racism.

Graffiti

Rebecca Partos

One day, when I was just under five, my sister, Hannah, and I went to a playground in Strawberry Hill. The sky was a beautiful shade of blue with little puffs of white clouds floating about. We played on the swings and the roundabout. It was fun letting the air gently breeze past us while we were whizzed about. Then we climbed up the green and orange ladder of the slide. Hannah sat on it and I pushed her, whooping as she quickly slid down.

There was a little house attached to the top. I climbed up and sat on the hut's floor. Gazing out of the window I could see a man sitting on the bench with a red nose from the October cold, glasses, a ridiculous bowler hat and moustache. Peering closer I noticed some words scribbled on the bench. Something like 'blaks stink'. I looked the other way: toddlers, screeching and cackling in the sandpit, parents swarming over them like bees to honey, children climbing the fence and kicking the red, yellow and orange autumn leaves, the muddy brown trees watching down, sadly, at the ground.

I looked at the wooden walls of the tiny house. There was a feast of graffiti all over, words like 'Sandy loves Blink' scrawled in sickly-pink spray-can. The word which fascinated me most was one written very jerkily in black. As I was so little I was still learning to read and I hadn't seen this word before. I read it aloud to myself, 'ni...ig...gggerr. Nigger.'. I traced the letters with my finger and then I heard Hannah yell from the trees near the private gardens.

'Rebecca! Come here!' I shuffled quickly down the steps and ran, half hopping and half running in that direction.

'Coming!' I replied and immediately forgot about the mysterious word. 'Look! I've found a baby hedgehog!' she whispered, crouched down by a pile of leaves. The hedgehog was asleep. Hannah was wearing a blue winter coat all buckled up, gloves and red trousers. She continued, 'Isn't it sweet? What shall we call her?'

'Harriet!' I said. 'But what if it doesn't have a mummy or daddy? I bet she's hungry.'

Then we saw a mother hedgehog and more little babies waddling along.

'Oh, she's all right then,' Hannah said.

After this we had a race to the seesaw. On the safety matting was another mark. 'Buz waz ere' one bit said and 'K...k...kill those bl...ack bas...tards!' I read.

'What does that mean?' my sister asked and looked up at me.

At home that evening I remembered the graffiti and asked my parents about them. They said those were very rude words for black people. That's when I discovered racism.

Four years later I was looking at the bookshelves at home when a title caught my eye. *Black Boy* by Richard Wright. I read the book and saw the horrors of racism in my mind like in a private cinema. Around the same time I found out more when I watched the news on television and heard about Stephen Lawrence, the black teenager who'd been murdered just because of the colour of his skin. I really felt sad for his family and I talked to mum about it. She told me about Nelson Mandela fighting for black people's rights in South Africa and how he had spent many years in prison.

It was only then that I began to understand how dangerous racism is. That's why I decided to give a talk in school about it. But I will never forget the first time I came across this terrible thing – through the graffiti on the playground.

Discussion points

After hearing the piece read aloud, read it to yourself a few times and discuss it with others.

The ability to read opens up the world – bad as well as good. The author has captured that loss of innocence, – when we first realise that people can suffer, or hate.

The powerful visual images – the people in the park, Harriet crouched over the hedgehog – contribute to the impact of this story. The 'rightness' of the playground and nature contrasts with the 'wrongness' of the hatred embodied in graffiti.

The power of racism is lessened when it is openly discussed, as when the author talked with her parents. If it is talked about, it can be condemned.

About the author...

Rebecca and her sister run a magazine called *Smart* for which they write stories, publish pieces by other children and interview their favourite authors. 'I like Jacqueline Wilson and Philip Ridley very much,' says Rebecca, 'and Benjamin Zephaniah is the most wicked poet in the world. We have a cooking page and do book reviews – I reviewed *Junk* (by Melvin Burgess). The incident actually happened four or five years ago and it stuck in my memory because I hate racism. I would like to be an artist or a writer.' At the time she wrote this story, Rebecca was a pupil at St Stephen's Primary School in Richmond, Surrey.

Rachel Busch

A Curious Journey

The nicest feet belonged to Calais and Zetes. They had little wings on each side of their ankles and they used to amuse themselves by fluttering their feathers for me to pounce on.

Mary Hoffman

There never was a voyage like it. I still remember it vividly, now I'm too old to do much except doze. Sometimes I can feel myself twitching in my sleep as I re-live one of our adventures.

When I first saw the Argo, I was afraid. Most of us don't like water and I'm no exception. But I'd been in little fishing boats to scavenge scraps of fish-heads so I knew you could stay on one and not get wet.

The Argo's huge prow towered above everything else in the harbour at Pagasae. There were 50 seats for oarsmen, but my master carried me on board before the crew arrived.

When they did take their places, I was too terrified to do anything but hide. I got used to them eventually, and soon learned which ones to steer clear of and which would give me scraps from their rations.

One of my favourites was Orpheus. He used to play on his lyre, when he wasn't rowing. And that was often very useful when the other sort of rowing started. They were a quarrelsome lot – like a lot of toms with too little territory to share.

Orpheus had a lovely voice and sometimes I just had to join in.

'What's that infernal caterwauling?' Hercules would say and look round for something to throw at me.

Hercules was *not* one of my favourites. He had the most enormous feet and he never looked where he was putting them.

The nicest feet belonged to Calais and Zetes. They had little wings on each side of their ankles and they used to amuse themselves by fluttering their feathers for me to pounce on.

'You should show more respect,' my master said. 'They are the sons of the North Wind and could send you flying if they wanted.' But they didn't. Only once I saw the other side of them.

We had landed in Thrace where our captain, Jason, wanted to consult the king about our route. King Phineus was supposed to be able to see the future.

I went on shore with the rest of the crew. We were still quite a long way from the palace when my sensitive nostrils caught the whiff of a terrible smell.

A sad scene awaited us in the palace. King Phineus was sitting at his banqueting table. He was thin to his bones yet what had once been a magnificent meal was spread before him. Most of it was being gnawed at by two hideous birds, with the faces of women. And what they weren't eating, they had fouled in the most revolting manner.

Braving the stink, I leapt up on to the table and gave chase to the filthy things. Calais and Zetes were right behind me and when the bird-women flew out of the window, the sons of the North Wind flew right after them!

They didn't come back for hours and then they told King Phineus that those Harpies would never bother him again. The whole party had moved to another room and we were now served a fine meal of roast lamb and honey-cakes. I got my share of scraps sitting under the table with my chin on the feathery ankles of my friends. It was almost as soft and comfortable as that fleece we had on the way home.

Ah, yes, that was a voyage to remember. I wonder if you've heard of it?

write away

About the author...

When asked how she gets ideas for her stories, Mary Hoffman says: 'I write out of compulsion – like Scheherazade in *The Arabian Nights*. Sometimes an idea comes with a title – *Amazing Grace* was like that. Sometimes a character invades the brain and lives with you. Sometimes a story grows out of an incident or something overheard. Some ideas arrive unbidden, others creep up gradually, more like stalactites. I do believe that the stories already exist, and I have to find a way of finding them and giving them life.'

Discussion points

After hearing the piece read aloud, read it to yourself a few times and discuss it with others.

The 'voice': Who is the narrator? When did you find out? What clues does the author give? Why do you think she has retold a Greek myth from the viewpoint of the ship's cat?What are the advantages of writing in the first person?

Description and detail: What sentences tell us things only a cat would describe?

Comments and judgments: Writers often include comments on their own and other people's behaviour. Find examples. Make a chart showing the main events in the left-hand column. In the middle column, match what the cat experienced in each event. In the right-hand column, write any comment or opinion the cat expressed.

Writing suggestions:

You may want to re-tell a story or myth from the viewpoint of a person, animal or thing. You may want to choose a story as a group and take different voices.

Try to imagine experiences through your character's eyes and decide how to describe them. Drama activities can help, such as acting a scene from the story, 'freezing', and asking the characters what they are feeling. Discussing how characters are portrayed can help you decide how they will behave and speak.

A planning chart – described above – may help when you are drafting. When you are redrafting, think about how well you are conveying the views of your 'voice'. Will readers know who is telling the story without your telling them?

Ted Dewan

He stuck two pieces of cotton on the bleeding parts and told me to bite hard. I almost bit them in half. As I left the room, he smiled at me. I felt like glaring.

The Day my Teeth Came Out

Nic Favaro

I've never had trouble with my dentist before. But after this experience I will never forget him again. I know what you're thinking. Having teeth out sounds pretty boring. It happens to everyone. But how I had them out? I don't think so.

I went to the dentist feeling so nervous. My knees were shaking. My heart was like a loud drum. I kept telling myself: 'It's OK, you'll be fine.' But I would never have agreed to having my teeth out if I had known what was about to happen.

There were children playing on the floor with toys, while I waited on the hard, cold chair. I envied them for their happiness. Most of them had probably never been to the dentist, let alone had a tooth out!

After 20 minutes – which felt like years – a sweet voice said, 'Favaro?'

My mum called, 'Yes.' Now my heart was really pounding. Like a 7.0 on the Richter scale. The assistant's smile looked fake. I shivered like I was in a blizzard. Then there was the squeaking of the door's rusty hinges, 'Eeeeeeeer.' I shivered again.

Inside, the new equipment twinkled in the sunlight. It looked more like Frankenstein's laboratory.

'Sit down, Nicolas,' said Dr Bolding.

I felt the chair sinking; I've always hated that part. The dazzling light blinded me. It was like having a million spotlights on me at once. 'OK. Let's begin.' I could have sworn there was pity in his voice.

I gulped. He shielded my eyes. I caught a glimpse of a huge syringe. I gulped again. He turned the light brighter so I couldn't see anything at all. The assistant held my hand and the dentist began his deed.

He pierced me on the right side of my top inner lip with the syringe (now this was unexpected!). I clutched the assistant's hand. It stung like a thousand bee stings. After a minute, he did the same on the left.

'This will sting a bit more,' he said after another minute. I gulped again.

Now he pierced me on my top right gum. I clutched the assistant's hand even tighter. He wasn't kidding. It hurt much more!!! Next he pierced me in my top left gum. 30 seconds went by and I wanted to stab him.

Now everything felt fat and numb from the inside of my mouth to my nose. I felt so stupid. Next, he turned the light down so that I could see for a change. Then he got out something that looked like a cross between a pair of tweezers and a wrench. He put it around my first canine. I thought, it won't hurt too much since everything is numb. Yeah, right.

He said, 'All you'll feel is a slight push on your tooth.' I could actually feel him wrenching it out. I clutched the assistant's hand so tight that I cut off her circulation. When the tooth finally came out I was feeling pretty rotten. Then he started on the next tooth. Ouch, ouch, ouch! I just wanted to SCREAM!!! That was it. I am never having another tooth out again.

After the second tooth came out, he stuck two pieces of cotton on the bleeding parts and told me to bite hard. I almost bit them in half. As I left the room, he smiled at me. I felt like glaring.

In the car, my mum asked me, 'Now that wasn't so bad, was it?'

The typical question every loving parent has to ask after the child has gone through something they thought was going to be the worst thing on earth.

I still had the cotton in my mouth and my lip was still numb so I couldn't really speak very well. I felt like saying, 'It wasn't bad, mum, IT WAS TERRIBLE!'

But all I managed was, 'Miph moph maf muf. Mif mof moffiflc!!!!'

Discussion points

After hearing the piece read aloud, read it to yourself a few times and discuss it with others.

Notice the opening lines. What makes us want to read on? Do you think Nic's experience was out of the ordinary?

The story is told with the intensity of personal experience, we share the sounds, sights and feelings of the author. How might it differ if it was told by the dentist or the assistant?

This story might remind you of a similar event. Recreate it in your mind: seeing, hearing, feeling what you experienced at the time. How will you engage the interest of the reader in your opening sentences?

About the author...

'It was a particularly memorable day,' said Nic, when he was subject to major orthodontic work: Wednesday 15th July 1998. 'If something can be made fun of, I do.' He has a full life. 'I play the piano and the cello and try to write for fun in my spare time, but the summer term is busy.' When he wrote this piece, he was a student at Claremont Fan Court, Esher, Surrey.

Rachel Busch

She smiled at me when she saw me hovering. Mum prodded me in the back and hissed at me to say something. I couldn't think of anything at all.

Jacqueline Wilson

I wonder if you've ever met anyone famous? I'll never forget the day I met Mandy Miller. She was a child actress when I was a little girl. I first saw her in a film called *Mandy.* You might just have seen it. It's on television every couple of years. I video it every time so I have several spare copies. It's still my favourite film.

Mandy plays a child who can't hear and can't speak. She's only about six, a sad chubby little girl with big dark eyes and long plaits. It's a dramatic emotional adult movie and I don't expect I understood all of it – but I fell in love with Mandy.

My mum found an article about her in *Women's Own* and cut it out for me. That was the start of my Mandy Miller scrapbook. Mum took me up to Wardour Street in Soho where the film companies were. They'd sometimes sell us stills from Mandy films, or even give us publicity photos as a present. Soho was an interesting place for a small girl but I didn't blink twice at the women in high heels on the street corners. I was too excited about collecting more Mandy pictures.

We ended up with many more photos of Mandy than we had of me. I kept them in a special suitcase and looked at them every single day. I was particularly fond of a hospital film where Mandy played a little girl called Jessie who was doomed to die. I had lots of photos of Mandy lolling in bed looking sad and stricken – and one funny photo where Mandy was being herself, sitting up in bed eating toffee and reading a *Lion* comic.

I liked these everyday pictures of Mandy most of all. I had several photos of Mandy's birthday party, Mandy blowing out her candles and then eating a huge slice of cake. I loved her smocked party dress but I liked her play clothes even more. She looked wonderful in dungarees swinging upside-down from a tree in her garden. My all-time favourite photo was Mandy sitting up in bed holding a lovely old edition of *Peter Pan.*

Mandy had everything I longed for. She had a sister, she lived in a big comfortable house with a garden, she had a poodle, she had lots of books, she had beautiful clothes, she had parties, she had ballet lessons, she had lovely long hair she could style into plaits or pony tails.

I didn't want to *be* her though. I just wanted to write about her. I filled a fat Woolworths exercise book with an official biography of Carmen Isabel Miller, popularly known as Mandy, but I got bored sticking to the facts. I had far more fun making up stories about Mandy-type girls, using my photos for inspiration.

Then one Easter my Mum read in the paper that lots of film stars were taking part in a special fun day at Battersea Park.

'You can meet Mandy!' she said.

I felt weirdly worried about this. It was too hot for me to wear my winter coat so I had to wear my grey school blazer which I hated. I had to wear my clumpy school sandals too. My short wispy hair had just been permed and stuck out alarmingly.

'I look awful!' I mumbled.

'You look very ladylike,' said Mum.

It was the *last* thing I wanted to look like. I wondered what Mandy would think of me.

'We probably won't even spot her,' said Mum.

I nearly did walk straight past her. I'd forgotten that my photos were years out of date. Mandy was well into her teens, so tall she towered over me – and all her lovely long hair had been cut almost as short as mine.

She smiled at me when she saw me hovering. Mum prodded me in the back and hissed at me to say something. I couldn't think of anything at all. Mum whipped out our Brownie camera and Mandy put her arm round me. I expect she felt me trembling. Then the photo was taken, Mandy said goodbye, waved and went off to sign autographs.

'There,' said Mum triumphantly. 'Happy now?'

I was. But somehow the real warm friendly girl wasn't quite the same as my imaginary Mandy. I was still a fan – but I stopped writing my Mandy stories, and the photos stayed shut in the suitcase, unthumbed for years.

Discussion points

The 'voice': Jacqueline Wilson writes directly to the reader as if she were speaking to you. How does she do this? From reading this account we learn a lot about Jacqueline Wilson as well as about Mandy Miller. What do you learn about her and why was she so taken with Mandy Miller?

Structure: This account is written with a clear structure. Notice how the writer establishes the situation: *I'll never forget the day I met Mandy Miller*. How does she then develop the account and bring it to its end?

Writing suggestions:

This account might remind you of something you used to care about or be interested in but aren't any more. It may also remind you of a situation where a person or an event did not live up to your expectations of it. Once you have thought about your own experience talk to a partner about it before you start writing. Plan the structure carefully as the author has done and try to speak directly to your reader.

write away

About the author...

When asked about her thoughts on reading and her own writing, Jacqueline Wilson says: 'Reading means so much to me that it gives me a real thrill to think that I might have helped children discover the joys of reading for themselves.'

Meeting Mandy

David Hitch

Goodbye Gran

Then it happened, the thing I had been dreading most came true.

Stephanie Cayzer

I was absolutely heartbroken. It was as if somebody had taken away part of my life, part of my history. I used to go there nearly every day of the week. We made egg and bacon quiches, picked flowers out of her small but beautiful garden. Then, as I grew older, I made up a bed on her two-seater settee, using her pillows and duvet from her single bed. I also used her settee cover, a beige-brown piece of cloth with fluffy material on one side. I attached it to the dark brown wooden trolley (which was in one corner of the room), stretched it over one of her chairs and rested it over the edge of the settee to use as the cover of a den. I covered up the entrance with a piece of sheeting. My den was furnished with Gran's pillows and a lovely purple, covered with white flowers, duvet. One reason why I loved her is that we had a lot of fun. We did so many things together.

It started about the end of June, 1997. She had this awful nose bleed and did not go to the doctors for six to eight weeks, and when she did go, the doctors thought it was a clot which could be easily removed, but further investigations showed it was a cancerous brain tumour.

After Christmas she had an operation to remove her tumour, in Derriford Hospital in Plymouth. Afterwards, for a few days, her nose and most of her face were covered in bandages. When I first saw her after the operation, I nearly burst into tears.

A little while after the operation, Gran came to the local hospital in Liskeard. She was there for a week or two before coming home for a while to spend time with her family (Mum, Dad and me).

I still went to visit her; we talked, we did a couple of crosswords together (in one of her many crossword books!). We also played Whist and watched some television. They were happy times, but, as days came and went, I could tell she would soon be dead; going to visit her was becoming more painful.

She then went back into the town hospital. It had not seemed so bad before as she had been in a room with other people but now she was in her own private room. At first she was awake when we went to see her but on Monday, the day before she died, she was sleeping like a baby. She was in a coma.

Then it happened, the thing I had been dreading most came true. Just after 4.35pm on Tuesday, March 24th, 1998, the hospital rang. Gran had died a few minutes earlier. I cried and cried and, when I went to bed, I cried again. What had Gran done to deserve such a horrid end?

I accompanied my parents to register Gran's death and visit her one last time, in her coffin. She looked so small and peaceful. I just wanted to hug her.

The funeral, which happened the following Monday, was really sad but I know Gran would have loved the flowers. I cried in the service and kept wishing I could bring her back, but now I realise that all the wishing in the world can't change anything.

Losing the one I love has changed my life the most. I still miss her. I love you, Gran.

Discussion points

After hearing the piece read aloud, read it to yourself a few times and discuss it with others.

This story is very moving, especially for readers who have experienced grief themselves. But, as the author says, writing can be helpful. It can help one grasp new understandings and come to terms with painful events – even if no one reads it but oneself. Writing can be an opportunity to 'talk it through' without anyone else hearing. But sharing it, as in this story, gives us all the chance to understand.

About the author...

Stephanie found writing this piece, 'painful, but a bit helpful'. Stephanie said the details were not too difficult to remember, 'because things like that stay in your mind,' but she did spend time re-drafting. She was a pupil at Liskeard Junior School, Cornwall when she wrote this.

Sarah Symonds

About the authors

Kit Wright

Kit Wright lives in East London. He writes for children and adults, broadcasts, gives poetry performances and runs writing workshops. His recent books include a retelling of *Rumpelstiltskin* in the Magic Beans series (Scholastic), and a new book of adult poems, *Hoping It Might Be So*, appears in October as part of his *Collected Poems* (Leviathan Press).

Raymond Briggs

Raymond Briggs has been writing and illustrating books for children for about 40 years. His best-known titles are *Father Christmas*, *The Snowman*, (Puffin) *When the Wind Blows* (Penguin), *Fungus the Bogeyman* (Puffin), *The Man*, *The Bear* (Julia Macrae) and the most recent is *Ethel & Ernest*, a strip cartoon biography of his parents. Some of these titles have been made into films and productions for the theatre.

Helen Cresswell

Helen Cresswell has written many critically-acclaimed books, some of which – *The Piemakers*, *The Bongleweed*, *The Night-watchmen* – have never been out of print. Her latest novel is *Snatchers* (Hodder). She is also a twice BAFTA nominated screenwriter and is adapting her own humorous series, *The Bagthorpe Saga*, for television.

Adèle Geras

Adèle Geras has lived in Manchester for the last 31 years. She is the author of more than 70 books for children and young adults. These include most recently the Cats of Cuckoo Square series (Transworld) and the Little Swan series (Red Fox). Her novel for teenagers, *'silent snow, secret snow'*, was published by Puffin in 1998, and David Fickling Books have just published a novel called *TROY*, which is also for older readers.

She has won the odd competition since the 1953 triumph described in her story.

Michael Rosen

Michael Rosen is 54 and is a successful poet, performer, scriptwriter and broadcaster. Both of his parents were teachers and they influenced his love of reading. He has a Master of Arts in Children's Literature from Reading University and a PhD from the University of North London.

Some of his publications include: *Quick Let's Get out of Here*, *You Wait Till I'm Older Than You* (Puffin), *We're Going on a Bear Hunt* (Walker), *Snore* (Collins) and *Michael Rosen's Book of Nonsense* (Hodder Children's). Forthcoming titles for this year are: *Centrally Heated Knickers* (Puffin) and *Even More Nonsense* (Hodder Wayland).

Mary Hoffman

Mary Hoffman has written over 70 books for children, including the best-selling *Amazing Grace* (Frances Lincoln 1991). She edits a quarterly magazine of children's book reviews, called *Armadillo*, and is a tireless campaigner for libraries.

Jacqueline Wilson

As an only child, Jacqueline Wilson was left to her own devices a lot of the time and she would play elaborate imaginary games for hours on end. She also 'wrote' many books, drew and read a lot. Her first job at 17 was on a teenage magazine and she had her first novel published when she was only 24. When she writes she uses a notebook and pen as she still hasn't learned to use a computer.

Rebecca Partos

Rebecca wrote this piece on a Write On! course, for children who want to learn the technicalities of writing, run by her mother, Vesna Pistotnik, but she is already an experienced author and editor. She goes to pottery classes and plays the piano.

Nic Favaro

Nic, who came to the United Kingdom from the United States when he was a year old, wrote his account of a painful visit to the dentist as a diary entry in the summer holidays. Nic has now gone back to live in Connecticut.

Stephanie Cayzer

Stephanie and her gran used to enjoy cooking and sewing together. Stephanie plays keyboards, writes stories for fun and enjoys reading, especially horror and adventure stories, and books by Philip Pullman and Lisa Daniels. She's good at maths as well.

Rosie Seager

Rosie has excelled in class writing assignments before. English is certainly one of her favourite subjects. Rosie also enjoys drama, has a sister at a local secondary school and a brother who has special needs.

Eimear O'Brien

Eimear, who has another sister and a brother, has had some previous success as a writer, including winning the BBC Young Journalist of the Year Award in 1995 when she was only nine. Her mother says Eimear was competing against 16-year-olds, so the family was surprised that her piece about a local badger sett in danger won the environment prize, and astonished that she won the overall prize. She has also won a W H Smith award for a story suggested by a news item about a boy in a coma.

Creative writing contacts

Arts Council of England
14 Great Peter Street
London SW1P 3NQ
Tel: 020 73330100
www.artscouncil.org.uk

Arts Council of Northern Ireland
MacNeice House
77 Malone Road
Belfast BT9 6AQ
Tel: 028 90385200
www.artscouncil-ni.org

The Scottish Arts Council
12 Manor Place
Edinburgh EH3 7DD
tel 0131 2266051
www.sac.org.uk

Arts Council of Wales
9 Museum Place
Cardiff
CF10 3NX
Tel: 029 20376500
www.ccc-acw.org.uk

Arvon Foundation
11 Westbourne Crescent
London W2
Tel: 020 72622788
www.arvonfoundation.org

British Educational Communications and Technology Agency (Becta)
Milburn Hill Road
Science Park
Coventry CV4 7JJ
Tel: 024 76416994
www.becta.org.uk

Book Trust
Book House
45 East Hill
London SW18 2QZ
Young Book Trust
Tel: 020 8516 2984
www.booktrust.org.uk

Centre for Language in Primary Education (CLPE)
Webber Street
London SE1
Tel: 020 74013382
www.clpe.co.uk

The English Association
University of Leicester
University Road
Leicester LE1 7RH
Tel: 0116 2523982
www.le.ac.uk/engassoc

National Association for the Teaching of English (NATE)
50 Broadfield Road
Sheffield S8 0XJ
Tel: 0114 2555419
www.nate.org.uk

National Association for Writers in Education (NAWE)
PO Box 1
Sheriff Hutton
York YO60 7YU
Tel: 01653 618429
www.nawe.co.uk

National Literacy Trust
Swire House
59 Buckingham Gate
London SW1E 6AJ
Tel: 020 78282435
www.literacytrust.org.uk

The Poetry Book Society
Book House
45 East Hill
London
SW18 2QZ
Tel: 020 88708403
www.poetrybooks.co.uk

The Poetry Society
22A Betterton Street
London WC2H 9BU
Tel: 020 74209880
www.poetrysoc.com

Reading and Language Information Centre
University of Reading
Bulmershe Court
Earley
Reading RG6 1HY
Tel: 0118 987 5123
www.ralic.rdg.ac.uk

United Kingdom Reading Association
1st Floor, Unit 6
The Maltings
Green Drift
Royston
Hertfordshire SG8 5DY
Tel: 01763 241188

Notes